MW01096826

Copyright© *2015*

ktucker@therealmspublishing.com
www.therealmsauthors.com

Best
Book
Ever

K.B. Tucker

To Ducky, you are 1/3 of My 'Why' and 100% of my heart.
To William, James and Nora: No matter what, Love Always.
That's The rule. That's The secret

In this book, there are NO pictures.

None?

Nada

Zip?

Z.I.L.T.C.H

ZILTCH

This is the most serious book in the WORLD!

Blehhhhh! Who wants that!?

Because...

On These very Pages...

There is...

a *Secret*...

A secret...
Secret

The Secret
is
Very
Very
Very
Secret

I'll give you One hint.

But No Giggling!

I wonder what the secret is?

I heard that!

You absolutely.
Cannot.
Even Smile.

Seriously...Or the Jig is UP!

Lauging is even Worse!!

I wonder what this secret is?

Please!

Shhhhhhhhhhhhhhhhhhhhhhhhhhhhhhhhhhhhhhhh

Please! Please! Please! Please! Please!
Please! Please! Please! Please! Please!
Please! Please!
Oh Pretty Pretty Gumdrop
with Sprinkles
and Speckles on Top!?

Contain Yourself! Or we can't keep going!

Whew!

Thank You

That was so

Pardon me!

As I was

HIC! HIC!

Sa...Hic...Sa Sa...HIC

Saying!

HICCUP!!

I'm sorry I have the hiccups

HIC!

Was THAT a Frog?

Did you Hear a TOAD?

Did

Those

Sounds

Come From Me?

Oh Me! Oh My!

OOOOOOOOHHHHH...

Wait a minute!!

This is a TRICK!!!

You!

How DARE You!

You! You!

Horrible

Gorrible

And Yet Still Strangely Huggable

Trickster!

You're Using the RULES Against me!
AAAANNND

The **Super Secret**

Of Books

(Including this Very book)

Revealed!!

How DARE You!

The Unmitigated

Gall

I don't even Know what that means!

I Thought
you
Liked Me!

But I have To...

By The Sacred Laws of Bookdom

(That's A bit Dramatic if you ask Me)

And My OATH as Battybumbum

Huh? Batty What What?

What was THAT?

I really don't like where this is going!

But I...

Must...

No Matter How

Super

Duper

McPooper

OR
Silly Billy
The Words Are

Oh...I said pooper!
Right there on that last page!!
I'm so Embarrassed!!!

This
Puckering
Purple
Pickle
Person

Has to read every word.
That's THE Secret!

THAT'S THE SECRET!
Oh No!

Every Single

Cablatious

Motatious

Fagratious

Bobatious

Until The Very Very End

Are We There Yet?
What Fresh....
Insanity is This?

Po.Ta.TIOUS
POtatoe Head

You're Killin' ME!
Hey....there is no 'e' in Potato

Toe in my Nose!
        Toe in my Nose!

I'm Just singing With my
Toe in my nose!

That's Disgusting!
Why would I even do that?
I certainly would not Sing About it!

Cause There's an 'E' in Toe
And it should be known that so
Does Nose!!

Oh I see...

Can we be done Please?

I Can't Take Any More!

Herby Derby Doooo!

Catch a Turkey By his Shoe!

Ok! Ok!
You WIN!!!
I totally give up.
Truce?

Shake On It?

Ppppppppffffffffftttttttttt!!

That was absolutely not my Idea!

The End

You are totally
Looney Bears if you
Think THAT was FUN!!
I'm NEVER Reading This Crazy Book Again!

Hic!

UtOh...!

Can You Survive

The secret...

Secret?

In THIS Book?

Made in the USA
Middletown, DE
15 September 2017